BUDDHIST
FESTIVALS AND TRADITIONS

by Sarah Shey

PEBBLE
a capstone imprint

Published by Pebble, an imprint of Capstone
1710 Roe Crest Drive, North Mankato, Minnesota 56003
capstonepub.com

Copyright © 2025 by Capstone. All rights reserved. No part of this publication may be reproduced in whole or in part, or stored in a retrieval system, or transmitted in any form or by any means, electronic, mechanical, photocopying, recording, or otherwise, without written permission of the publisher.

Library of Congress Cataloging-in-Publication Data is available on the Library of Congress website.
ISBN: 9780756594657 (hardcover)
ISBN: 9780756594701 (paperback)
ISBN: 9780756594695 (ebook PDF)

Summary: Readers curious about world religions can explore the meaning and customs behind major Buddhist holidays and festivals, including Vesakh, Asalha Puja, and the Buddhist New Year.

Editorial Credits
Designer: Dina Her; Media Researcher: Jo Miller; Production Specialist: Tori Abraham

Image Credits
Alamy: Godong, 15, John Vincent, 13; Getty Images: dangdumrong, 5, Natnan Srisuwan, 1, 11, picture alliance, 29, Richard Baker, 25, TaManKunG, 19, thipjang, 21; Shutterstock: Attitude, background (throughout), Firmansyah Asep, 8, godongphoto, 10, Jasper Neupane, 23, Jaynothing, 22, kawee su, 28, NullPixel, 27, Ohishiapply, 20, PBXStudio, cover (bottom), saravutpics, cover (top), Tungalag Balzhirova, 17, Vietnam Stock Images, 7

Any additional websites and resources referenced in this book are not maintained, authorized, or sponsored by Capstone. All product and company names are trademarks™ or registered® trademarks of their respective holders.

Printed and bound in the USA. 6121

TABLE OF CONTENTS

Introduction to Buddhism 4

Vesakh 6

Asalha Puja 12

Buddhist New Year 18

Life Events 24

The Vihara and the Monastery 28

    Glossary 30

    Read More 31

    Internet Sites 31

    Index 32

    About the Author 32

Words in **bold** are in the glossary.

INTRODUCTION TO BUDDHISM

Buddhism began with a prince on a quest. Prince Siddhartha Gautama was born in present-day Nepal sometime between 563 and 483 BCE. That was about 2,600 years ago.

In India, Siddhartha **meditated** under a tree for 49 days. Finally, he reached **enlightenment**. He now understood the truths of suffering. He taught those truths so others could suffer less. His students called him Buddha.

Today, Buddhism is the fourth-largest religion. Most Buddhists live in Asia. But they can be found all over the world. Each country celebrates holidays differently. Some even hold them on different days.

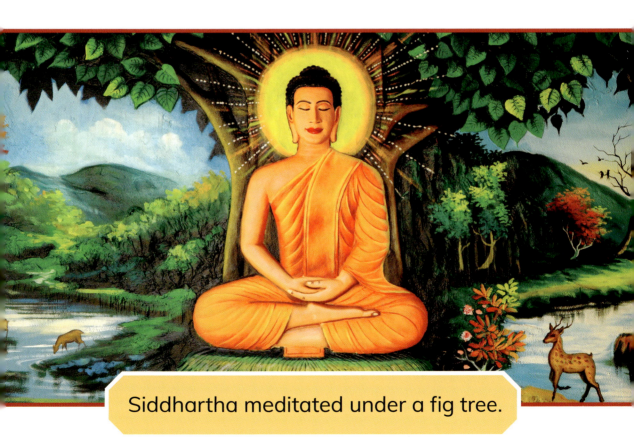

Siddhartha meditated under a fig tree.

VESAKH

In many places, Buddha's birthday is celebrated during May's first full moon. Some countries in Southeast Asia honor Buddha's awakening and death on the same day as well. These joint holidays are called Vesakh, or Buddha Day.

On Vesakh, Buddhists do good deeds. They offer food to others. People bathe Buddha statues and offer them food and flowers. Some decorate temples with lotus flowers made from paper. Lotuses grow out of mud to bloom above the water's surface. They symbolize spiritual awakening.

Lotus flowers remind people that everyone has the potential to reach enlightenment.

Every year, thousands of monks gather at Borobudur for Vesakh.

There are special Vesakh celebrations at Borobudur in Indonesia. This is the world's largest Buddhist temple. Buddhists walk along the road to the temple with **clergy** called monastics. They carry offerings for Buddha such as candles, flowers, fruit, and **incense**.

Offerings are symbols of Buddha's teachings. They are placed at the main **altar**. Both Buddhists and monastics pray together. They march three times around the temple to honor the Three Jewels, which are vows Buddhists make.

The Three Jewels are the heart of Buddhism. The first Jewel is Buddha, the first teacher. The second is the Dharma, Buddha's teachings. Finally, Sangha represents the community and all living beings.

A Buddhist symbol with dots that stand for The Three Jewels.

Many Buddhists spend all day and all night at their local temples.

When the sun goes down, people write their prayers and hopes onto paper lanterns. These are released into the sky. The glowing lanterns symbolize releasing negative thinking. They are also a reminder to do better.

ASALHA PUJA

Asalha Puja celebrates Buddha's first public teaching. Some traditions observe it in July.

This first teaching is important because it started Buddhists on the path to end suffering. Buddhists all over the world go to temples to hear monastics recite Buddha's words. Buddhists practice generosity and make offerings to monastics and Buddha statues.

Buddhists bring offerings and light candles in Thailand.

Buddha's first teaching was about the Four Noble Truths. The truths say that suffering means being in pain. If suffering is seen and understood, it can be let go. Letting go of suffering leads to happiness.

This path to end suffering is known as the middle path. It tells Buddhists that they can reach a state of peace and freedom that has no suffering. This state is called **Nirvana**.

Buddhist monastics guide people through Buddha's teachings.

Tibetan people call this holy day Chokor Duchen. It is observed on June 4. On this day, good deeds mean even more. Tibetans gather and hear Buddha's teachings. Poor people are given food, and animals in markets are freed. People light butter lamps to ask for wisdom and to push away darkness.

Altar offerings include fruit, flowers, and small dough and butter sculptures called torma. A common torma is decorated with a sun, a moon, and a lotus flower. Colorful prayer flags blow in the breeze, symbolizing good fortune flowing to all.

Butter lamps traditionally use clarified yak butter called ghee.

BUDDHIST NEW YEAR

The Buddhist New Year is a time to start again. Some countries celebrate the new year for three days after April's first full moon. Others celebrate on the first day of the first month of the **lunar calendar**, which is in January or February.

In some traditions, young people give thanks to their elders on the first day of the New Year. Elders give new year blessings. Children wash their elders' hair and hands and cut their nails.

Young people pour water over the hands of their elders to show respect.

Millions of people in Southeast Asia participate in water fights.

In some Southeast Asian countries, Buddhists cannot celebrate the new year without getting wet! Songkran, the Water Throwing Holiday, cleanses the old and welcomes the new. In Myanmar, it is called Thingyan. It lasts for four or five days from the end of March into April.

Water is cleansing. It is also a prayer for a good harvest. For days, people splash each other in community water fights. They dance in flooded streets. Even Buddha statues get a respectful water bath.

Clean or scented water is used to cleanse Buddha statues.

The new year is a time to give and receive blessings. Older people go to the temple to fast, meditate, and hear Buddha's teachings. Monastics and the statues receive offerings of rice, noodles, and fruit.

Monks collect offerings in special vessels called alms bowls.

A plate of khapse with glasses of Tibetan butter tea

A sweet year is wished for with sweet treats. Tibetans eat deep-fried butter khapse cookies. In Myanmar, they eat a semolina cake with coconut cream called sanwei makin.

LIFE EVENTS

In many countries, monastics bless newborns. There may be a special naming **rite**. Parents promise to raise the child as a Buddhist.

In Nepal, a local religious teacher called a lama offers prayers for the baby. A great lama called the Rinpoche chooses the baby's name. The Rinpoche cuts a little of the newborn's hair, picks a name, and gives their blessing.

Some children's parents ask the **Dalai Lama** for blessings. These children are given his personal name.

A Tibetan Buddhist lama blesses a baby.

Death is seen as a great teacher. Most Buddhists believe in rebirth. Rebirth means the person is recycled and changed in some way.

Monastics often play a central role at funerals. Chanted **scriptures** and prayers help the dead on their journey. Prayers comfort the living and offer connection with the dead.

Buddhists often pray special mantras near the dying. These words encourage positive thoughts as people die. It is important to connect with Buddha and have good thoughts in the last minutes of life.

Buddhist monks often lead funerals.

THE VIHARA AND THE MONASTERY

Male and female monastics have always been part of Buddhism. Monastics teach the Dharma. They learn chants and rituals. In some places, monastics don't cook or work. Instead, regular people give them food and money.

Offerings are given to make sure that monastics have enough to eat.

Children at a Myanmar vihara

Buddhist children in some countries join a **vihara** for a short time. Some join to bring honor to their family. Others join to learn Buddha's ways. In Myanmar, becoming a monastic helps rural and poor boys and girls become educated. The children learn that they can be like Buddha too.

GLOSSARY

altar (AHL-tuhr)—a table or platform to hold and present religious offerings

clergy (KLUR-jee)—a person who carries on religious work

Dalai Lama (DAH-lay LAH-muh)—the highest spiritual leader of Tibetan Buddhism

enlightenment (en-LIE-tuhn-mehnt)—the experience of awakening to reality

incense (IN-sens)—material that produces a strong smell when burned

lunar calendar (LOO-nur KAL-uhn-dur)—a calendar based on the cycles of the moon

meditate (MED-i-tayt)—to relax the mind and body with breathing patterns and mantras that help concentration

Nirvana (nur-VAH-nuh)—a state of happiness without suffering that does not end

rite (RYT)—an action performed as part of a religious ceremony

scripture (SKRIPT-shur)—sacred religious writings

vihara (vuh-HAH-ruh)—a Buddhist monastery

READ MORE

Andrews, Elizabeth. *Buddhism*. Minneapolis: DiscoverRoo, an imprint of Pop!, 2024.

Layton, Christine. *Travel to China*. Minneapolis: Lerner Publications, 2022.

Sanche, Heather. *The Life of the Buddha*. Boulder, CO: Bala Kids, an imprint of Shambhala Publications, Inc., 2020.

INTERNET SITES

Buddhism for Kids: Buddhist Holidays & Festivals
buddhismforkids.net/holidays.html

UNESCO World Heritage Convention: Lumbini, the Birthplace of the Lord Buddha
whc.unesco.org/en/list/666/

United Religions Initiative: Buddhism: Basic Beliefs
uri.org/kids/world-religions/buddhist-beliefs

INDEX

Asalha Puja, 12

babies, 24, 25

Buddha, 4, 6, 9, 10, 12, 14, 15, 16, 21, 22, 26, 29

Buddhist New Year, 18, 20, 22

Dalai Lama, 24

Dharma, 10, 28

enlightenment, 4, 7

food, 6, 16, 22, 23, 28

Four Noble Truths, 14

funerals, 26, 27

lotuses, 6, 7

monastics, 9, 12, 15, 22, 24, 26, 28, 29

monks, 8, 22, 27

Nirvana, 14

offerings, 9, 12, 13, 16, 22, 28

Sangha, 10

temples, 6, 9, 11, 12, 22

Three Jewels, 9, 10

Vesakh, 6, 8, 9

ABOUT THE AUTHOR

photo credit: Courtyard Photography

Sarah Shey is a writer and a librarian. She is grateful to all the Buddhists who so generously agreed to be interviewed. While Buddhism has influenced her life, Shey respectfully acknowledges that she is only a cultural mediator between Buddhism and the readers of this book.